I Hope You Fall in Love

R YS Perez

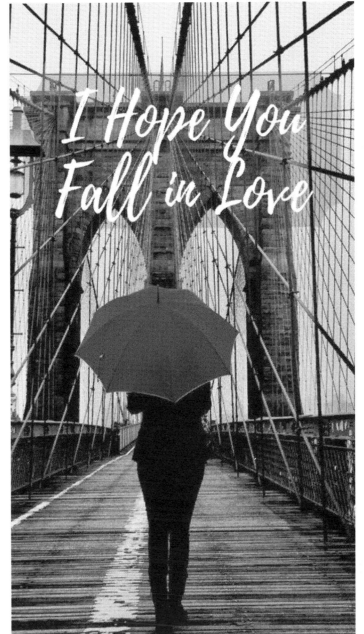

I Hope You Fall in Love

This book is for many people;

For my parents and grandparents,
who encouraged my love of reading and
writing

For Roland,
who did not get to see this book come to be

For Anastasia,
Who I am so proud of

For Henry

But most importantly,
for those who love hard, and those who are
afraid to.

CONTENTS

Introduction

I seem to have a problem when it comes to writing: I only seem to write when I am either falling in love or falling apart. I have become acutely aware of the pain that resides in my chest when I cannot hold myself together even when my arms are wrapped around myself. I am intimately acquainted with the pain of falling apart. And so instead, when you write, I hope you fall in love.

I have had this idea that writing is all about divergent thinking colliding with a hurricane of emotions. Perhaps this is why I find myself in this predicament when it comes to my writing. As a writer I must be capable of putting names to my demons, give details to the sound of leaves under my feet, and correlate each feeling to one another into a new kind of understanding. I must have access to vast terminology that can give names to everything I am trying to say. I must be capable of stringing syntax together to evoke empathy in both myself, as the writer, and the reader as we unravel my words. But without overflowing emotions what could possibly bend us to the will to write so intensely? I find the most powerful thing about language is its capability to express our pain and our hearts. While we can wear our sorrow and shoulder our pain we may never keep going without hope. For the past decade I have found my hope and tears at the tip of my pen. However, I found my love in the micro spaces between laced fingertips.

I have always tried to understand why I write when I am falling in love. If by writing I could not make any more sense of it then why was I writing about it? Why was I trying to express something that not only has infinite stockpiles of written works on it, but something that could never truly be expressed completely? It is horrifying to think, after thousands of years of literature, poetry, music and written words, everything has already been said. What more could I possibly add to the idea of love that is revolutionary? I only understood why I wrote about love when I rushed to find paper to write on. They are words that need to be said, to be expressed, and the only way I know how is the best way I can: to do so as a writer.

I found a journal I misplaced a month ago, and as I scanned through the pages I had written on I see snippets and lines of poetry and musings. Reading these lines I was reminded of something I had forgotten in my attempts to understand why I wrote about love. Love is chaotic, that is the secret. We can be as verbose as we so choose or eloquently describe every lingering feeling, but it will never rise to the unruly control love has on us. When you write about love, when you are in love, you lose control. You forget to protect yourself for one moment and then forever fear being hurt because it is out of your hands now. The secret is love is a chaotic mess of every emotion we humans have given a name to. Love no longer becomes a feeling - it becomes a storm. We write about love because it has become our favorite form of making the most out of life. Therefore, you should fall in love as often as you can. Fall in love with a thing, with a soul, with every person in your life. Fall in love with your very existence. Only then will you know you have lived.

So, in those moments of joy, and the moments you cry, I hope you write. When your lover has made you angry or flustered, and fall to pieces, I hope you write. When the ones you love are far away; when the ghost limb of them tries to move, when you wake from a dream you wish would come true, I hope you write. I want you to write the simple moments; the way the curve of their lips curl at the corners, the serenity in their silence, or the weight of their sigh. I want you to write of every heartbreak, every hospital visit, every firework. May you take note of the days as they pass, and thanks be to whatever had to happen for you to be where you are in your life. I hope through it all, you write. Most of all, for every reason you write, I hope you fall in love.

3 November 2015

My goal in a novel is to create the "Manic Pixie Dream Girl" and break her stereotype. No longer will she be used as a tool to propel the plot of the male lead. The Manic Pixie Dream Girl will have her own story, because she has things to say, too.

The Portrait

I knew exactly what I wanted when I asked him to draw it for me. I did not take the commission lightly, even if it was my best friend; he is the artist and I am the dreamer. I expected it to be exactly as I imagined. There was no remorse over the eraser shavings, hardly a batted eye at all the drafts scattered over the tables. We spent days in all these odd places; I sat there unmoving while trying to read without blocking my face as he sat there sketching my face over and over again. In the end, it is still unfinished.

She now rests in the porthole on the wall, staring at me sometimes, but she watches me more intently from my thigh. She is painted there between the layers of skin in the way I imagined her. Upon the wall she is a traveler in time, a mixture of what was and will be. On my skin her hand presses against her barrier, trapped in the past, Alice behind a glass. I keep her there separate from me.

When I first imagined her I knew who she was, and I knew her well. With her sad eyes, and her heavy presence, she was someone who was haunted. She rests on my skin as a reminder. She stares as a reminder of where I have been. She is the reminder I need of heartaches, heartbreaks, and tears I have shed. She whispers to me the times I will never return to, and the mistakes I will not replicate.

Most of all, the girl in the frame, the lost, sad little girl is taking strides to becoming who she always wanted to be. Colorful, buoyant, witty. Alive. Thank you, to her, for reminding me how far I have come. Thank you to the artist, for bringing her to life. Thank you, time, for continuing with or without me.

The Art of Falling Apart

The theory of the tormented artist, the idea that the torture of one's soul is the master creator, has given way to the conclusion that you can never create when you are happy. As a writer I have not only seen this theory being stereotyped, but I have seen it, and I have experienced it. During times of happiness I have found myself incapable of being able to write, when not a single word escapes my imagination. Times when there is a drought of joy and the words and letters simply pour out, a syntactical escape between my soul and pen. Angry at the stereotype, I have spent hours frustrated and stumbling over blank and cluttered pages, trying futilely to express the beaming joy from night lights and bumping music. Instead, after my fist fights with my vernacular, I am left dissatisfied with a piece I am ashamed of. For a long time I was irritated with my incapability to write about my happiness.

Magic only seemed to occur when there were pieces of me trying to break apart and splatter on the page.

Thank the muses, falling apart comes in many faces. There are many different parts of me to paint on a page. I have realized that the common misconceptions, the default examples, when we think of falling apart are breakups, heartbreaks, and death. Through writing, through the tightness in my chest, I have learned those are not the only times I needed to put myself back together again. When my veins pulse with rage my words would assault the page, the protest crying out when injustice leaves a bitter taste I cannot stand. Trauma has caused more than haunting backstory to be told, but brought along the anxiety I try to scratch off my skin in a jumbled mass of illegible script.

Words are enchanted. When I turned to my words I found a way to communicate the things I found hard to put a name to. In my journals I found therapy for a mind too afraid to get lost in the madness. My words where the cursive route to finding myself, and I'm still following their path. Healing is the gift writing brings to the pandemonium is falling apart. It has become apparent that falling apart has become the best prompt.

It's been said Van Gogh ate his yellow paint, because he saw yellow as a personification of joy, and he consumed it to try to get the happy inside of him. While this was later proven to be a myth, I believe, in the same way, we all have our nonsensical ways of trying to put all the pieces of ourselves back together. I was gluing the cracks with words, so it made no sense to try to force diction when I am happy. Jubilance was meant to be revealed in. When words failed I realized there was something unspeakably beautiful in not being able to put words to your happiness.

30 April 2016

I refer to people as being made up of tiny pieces because we create them, we build them, we leave them behind, and too often they fall apart. The beauty lies in being able to put them back together again.

Starlit Raindrops On Sidewalks

There is a distinct freedom in the air,
the smell of burnt sugar laced with the
lingering crisp of vibrant leaves.
City of glass, city of missing angels - the
city where he came to be.
The cry of time weeping across the sky.
There are nights like this where the
sidewalk reflects the coming snow;
and the stories of old dance a strange line
between the silent pauses of our heart beats.

He takes on the world with his gloves up,
but his heart still attached,
giving himself the chance to pull at the

strings with every hit.
Fireflies twinkle in the midnight,
neon and florescent shining in his eyes.
He is open with life,
and takes only what he makes.
He wears his experiences
woven into his demeanor -
the challenges, the pain,
the readiness to keep going.
He was the flavor of vinegar and sweets -
a sharp surprise and a deep satisfaction.

Her appearance in his life
slows him down,
and for the first time in a long time
his body melts into relaxation.
Her small frame caving in on the world;
the weight a feather is enough
to knock her broken self down.
She tasted of coffee and day old poetry.
Her words healed her aching heart as they
bled on the page,
sealing them in an envelope with a
hopeful band aid,
his touch a graze that kisses every scar.

As the day arrives the magic remains
unbroken with the song birds,
where she once thought every
imperfection would disperse it all.
She leans toward him –
a flower tilting in the morning sun.

Some wounds will never heal,
some wounds will come to be,
but by his side
she will take each of them gladly.

Some miracles,
some magic,
does not end when tomorrow comes.
Even in the daylight
she was surprised
by their chance meeting.
We are all lost,
but somehow
he had found
her in the chaos.

Words

He told me my talent was not writing, it
was words. I was surprised to realize I had
never thought of it that way myself. I had
liked to believe I was an extrovert, in the
way I connected with people, in my friendly
being, in my need to dance away the silence,
but I have learned in many ways I am not.
Too often I found myself eerily in the
background of a group, all the times I
hesitated to speak up, and even the way I
refused to call in to order take out. These are
simple ways my silence has given me pause,
however it is in the ways that my silence
wounds me that has become too much to

bare.

Few understand the sensation of choking on a word, each syllable getting caught in your throat, bringing tears to your eyes because you just want it out, you want to be rid of the thing that leaves the lump inside of you. Your vocal cords are a knotted mess, and you are unsure if you were taught to be this way, or if you have gained these insecurities through people who demanded you were meant to be seen and not heard. This world was meant to be for wallpaper women, what good was wallpaper that speaks?

He told me to describe a kiss, and I whined and wanted to hide. I hid within myself and I tried to pull lines from mind to lips. My mind was a mess, and I found it hard to think. Panic seems to press a button that throws all the files in your brain up in the air. It took more than a few tries, and it took a lot of pain to even look him in the eye. To speak and be seen at the same time was new for me. Everything was too; too raw, too much, too serious, too singular of a moment. I wanted too many more.

I want to write what my answer was, but I do not think it is enough anymore. Words on paper are no longer enough, not alone at least. I want to find my voice. I want to describe many more kisses with him, and tell him how each one of them felt.

My sister asked me "Do you love someone all the time?" And it was one of those moments when I realized I could say something profound. So, I took a deep breath, thought about it. No, I said, sometimes you'll want to strangle them more than you love them. But then it passes, and you'll love them even more.

Borderlines & Twisted Tongues

One day, when I was traveling on the train in the underground of Gotham City, there was a small band of Native Americans were performing a musical number and I had stopped to watch for a few minutes. As I was walking away the lead singer pulled away from his makeshift stage and called out after me. As I turned to face him he rested the pad of his thumb in the center of my forehead and asked if I was Native like he was. I told him I am not. He stared at me in the eyes for a long moment before resting his hand on my shoulders and told me it did not matter. He told me I should understand and connect with my ancestors no matter where they are from; and if I do that then I am still very much like him and his culture. I don't think I will ever forget that moment.

It was then, for the first time, I understood how important it is to know your own history. Never before had I thought that it should matter, after years of experiencing nothing but negativity from people who took such importance to origin. I realized how important where you are from is to our own personal story.

When I was younger I would sit at the edge of my great grandmother's bed, and to this day I cannot tell you how, with neither of us speaking the same tongue, we sat for hours talking and sharing M&M's. I sat there at the table and watched my *Abuela* cook meals, the ones she missed from back on the island, and be able to share that experience of "grandma's cooking" with every other Hispanic I came into contact with since. I could tell you of the years my grandfather spent listening to me trip over simple phrases from his native tongue, and all I wanted to do was break up the words into little pieces so that they would never hurt me again.

Only now that I am older do I understand my grandmother's need to know where she comes from stems from the same branch of her need to constantly photograph our family. It is so we ourselves will always have a history. She never wanted any of us to grow up forgetting what it was all about.

My family is like America; we are a blend of melanin and uncertain borders. There is no absolute answer to where we end and our country begins. In our country I can be a confusing entanglement of many cultures, be proud of every single one, and still wake up and be only who I am. Individualism is ruling, but the undercurrent of something more, something greater, of something that is patriotic - and feels much more like home - is really what governs these lands.

My Family is like America; from Alphabet City's creativity and originality, to the conservative and old fashion ways of Iowa. We are young and old blending together on Floridian state lines, Disney World and gated communities. We are as bright as California, frigid as Main. You can go across the country and be in awe at the fact that we are even in the same lands.

My Family is like America; a country of tolerance, and so many other things all at once. A beautiful mess of so many complexities. My Family is like America; or at least the America I would like to be in.

On Anxiety

Let me tell you about panic attacks:
They start by feeling so very much like a
heart attack.
You will think you are dying but the end just
won't come fast enough.
When you live with anxiety disorder some
days are a lot harder than others.
My anxiety takes different forms;
Sometimes it is manic,

It is moving,
It is not being able to get the words out fast enough.
It is wanting to crawl out of my own skin.
Sometimes,
it is not being able to c r a w l out of the bed
in the morning.
When I meet people I give them a warning:
I am a war,
And I have become a battlefield
that never sees peace.
Take me as I am.

You are the first thing to ever fully be
capable of calming me.
I am still unsure if I like that.
I have had enough people ripped from my
smile,
who have been tattooed

as birds
on my back as reminders,
people are not home.
I refuse to be homeless.
I am my own house,
and I shake enough to keep me standing and
knowing that I am alive.
I am decorated with wounds and worry,
I try to be quiet, I try to be brave,
But I cannot escape my suffering,
and I gave no one the key.
Despite all the warnings,
and the locked doors,
I still don't know how I have come to find you
here.
I wonder sometimes
if you can feel me
c r u m b l e
beneath your fingertips,
I wonder if you are ever burned
by the raging flames
I am made of.
I want to be okay.
But sometimes I think,
Perhaps,
in the beginning,

when we were all made of stardust
I just never stopped exploding.
You want to be there for me
But an anxiety attack is a
solitary
activity.
I spent years clawing at this body.
I've stayed awake all night,
fighting demons,
trying to figure out a way to tell you
there are parts of me hidden in closets.
The skeletons whisper to me there,
Telling me the world will end
over and over again.
Yet every day I will wake up to live in
agonizing anticipation.
I seek more than a shoulder to cry on,
I seek more than a kind world.
It is not the world that hurts me;
It is myself.
You watch me,
waiting in horror for me to collapse;
But, darling, I need you to know,
you loving me will not heal me.
Please realize, I already know that.

And I do not expect it to.

Under My Pillow

Every night I go to sleep with a shelf worth on my bed. There is an unfinished copy of Jane Eyre resting somewhere between the sheets, and she whispers to me the story I already know by heart. From my bed I face the tall shelf with tiers of books, a wedding cake marrying me to my love of reading.

Sleeping with books is not something unfamiliar to me. I have laid with many heroes, and begrudgingly kept awake by villains of all sorts. Scout Finch reminisces her childhood, Kit Tyler dreamily describes Nat, and Marina Keegan speaks beyond the grave. It's said a reader never goes to bed alone, and I firmly believe that, because night after night I am faced with each

21

character in my bed, awaiting the continuation of their tales. Across from where I lay, my baby Alice sits there in a pout, feeling cheated. Her rabbit hole is waiting for me again, and I have differing options to take down, down, down. Where The Hatter and the grin without a cat are frozen in time awaiting for tea.

Tonight I found comfort in the familiar words of Snicket, my eagerness for the story to come to life is only conquered by my consistent re-reading. Under my pillow, however, is the story of the Baudelaires continues as I dream pass the closing of the books. Klaus extending his hand for his fellow booklover, as we all run from the vile Count Olaf.

Sleeping with books is a vicious affair, I do not believe it will ever stop. Thankfully, my lover understands, for we both find our company doubled in bodies and pages. Is it not a wonderful thing, to find these stories haunting us in the middle of the night?

Between Heartbeats

She
sat down for a few
moments, and walked about
the room, but said
not a word. After a silence of several
minutes, thus began:
"In vain I have struggled.
My feelings will not be repressed. You
must allow me to tell you I
love you."

coloured, doubted,
silent

but

more

tender   .

dwelt on

wounding,

.

she lost all   passion
. She tried,   to compose
herself   with patience

which
had found impossible
with   hope that it
would   be   acceptance

apprehension and anxiety,

the colour rose into her
cheeks, and she said:
"   I believe,
the
obligation for the sentiments   ,

24

But I
cannot

hope
feelings which
have long

difficulty in overcoming
."

eyes fixed on her face,
seemed to catch her

complexion
became pale

struggling for calmness .

26 December 2016

The beautiful thing about writing is that I can have second chances. This time I can be better. This time it can be wonderful. This time I can be enough.

I Knew a Girl

I knew a girl who grew up being the type of woman men liked to fall in love with. They swore her face was sweet, sprinkled perfectly with connect the dot freckles they all hoped spelled out their name. As she grew older, her curves that bent in and faded out made them take a look at her just one more time. Boys, who in reality had no idea what the future held, would take a glance at her and etch the word forever in their retina and perfect in flesh colored ink across her skin. Every man watched her butterfly down the street like she was their own personal five foot promise.

Growing up she had boys come up to her to befriend her with other thoughts in mind. Still she would take them in and allow them to set camp in her eyes and visit her soul. Welcoming them all too willingly than she now admits she should have. She started thinking about her wedding at the age of seven and by seventeen she had everything figured out. All she was waiting for was a groom; a man who would be happy to pin his last name to hers.

But I once knew a girl who grew up using men's feelings as life rafts, hoping they would save her from the unwanted attention of her attacker. She was trying to drown his touch in a sea of fingertips; only to realize they all feel the same on her skin. Making her feel dirty and used, she tried to pretend it did not bother her, while she let each passing man through her life pretending she did not wish for them to be the one to finally say he will stay. The weight of the world had become the weight of her sheets.

Growing up she would look for affection constantly, constantly needing to feel like she was being used for more than her womanhood and body heat. She always wanted to feel like she was in control, tired of being the tires screeching on rainy highways. She wanted to be more than the lost girl looking for sympathy, she wanted to be what he was looking for. But that never seemed to be enough.

Growing up she had become used to allowing men the ability to curve themselves into question marks around her and hold her desperately as if she were the answer. She had become afraid to admit she is not. She has, instead, become a problem manifested and metastasizing, bubbling into a mass of compliments and excuses. And not one person would notice the grey parts of her until it was too late, because everyone falls for a pretty face.

She is a woman configured into messy thoughts, a bundle of nerves, a lovely face- a novel waiting to be published and shared- who releases her breaths onto empty pages. She is not made of metaphors, she is not a living poem. She is a woman, with bruised skin stretched over aching muscles and splintered bones. And as more time passes the less it seems to matter these two girls are both the same person.

If I Should Have A Daughter

My dearest daughter,
they will place you in my arms with a
blanket swaddling you,
And I will lay your head on my chest
Like a warm blanket
in the dead of winter.
You, and the grip of your tiny hands,
Will save me with a reason to believe
God still gives second chances.

My daughter, there will be times when
you feel like an ant in a giant's land,
Afraid, but far too curious to back down.
There will be days where you will find
Everything bright and colorful,
Until the next, when you will
Find it scary and hostile;
And that is when

I will be there for you the most.
I will be there at 2 a.m.
When you cannot sleep
From nightmares haunting you,
And there at 3 in the afternoon
When all you want to do is dance.
You will grow up with
Disney, superheroes,
And the unexpected.
Muñeca,
You will be whimsical, rebellious
And everything I am not.
Be strong willed, confident,
And full of faith.

Perhaps, in only a few things
You will be like your mother;
Unforgiving clumsiness, overly emotional,
Full of imagination, and biting wit.
And just when I would think you have
Inherited nothing from your father
I will witness you walk
With your head held high,
Command a room,
And charm everyone you meet.
Those will be the moments
When I will smile and say:
"There he is."

My daughter,
You will have malt chocolate eyes,
And a smile that will make hearts race.

Your beauty will be in
Shades of melanin and light.
On the backs of your hands I will write
Every way you are beautiful,
So that you may never forget.
Please, never forgive me if
I do not tell you enough.

I want you to know that your first kiss
Will be awkward,
With teeth
You won't know what to do with.
And your first time will be
Even more embarrassing,
Full of clumsy motions and hesitation.
Your first love will be like the sun,
Your last will happen without notice.

Remember broken hearts cannot be
Patched with band aids,
Filled in with empty promises,
Or mended with needle and thread.
Know that
Only love and time will heal you -
And sometimes
You have to make both of them
On your own.

This world will try to break you,
Do not let it.
You are young and a woman,
and so many will try

To make these the reasons to not give you
What you deserve.
As my daughter,
I expect you to demand it, work for it, and
Take it all by force.
Make everything you deserve on your own.
There is nothing people fear more these days
Than strong woman.

My darling,
I cannot teach you everything,
Nor will I ever feel as though
I have prepared you enough for this world.
Please know that will fail frequently,
And I do not have all the answers.
Just remember
Your mother is a writer,
And your father, he's a fighter.
And you are the baby girl
With big eyes, and a small frame,
who will always plant her feet and
Live without apologizing.

12 June 2015

I have never been drawn to luxury. I love the simple things; coffee shops, books, and people who try to understand.

Eloquent

"If your everyday life seems poor, don't
blame it; blame yourself; admit to yourself
that you are not enough of a poet to call forth
its riches; because for the creator there is not
poverty and no poor, indifferent place."
- Rainer Maria Rilke, *Letters to a Young Poet*

Every day I watch the way the sun rises in
the sky, I take notice of the pale yellow of the
painted walls, and inhale the grass's cry of
the early morning. You see, I fall in love with
the simple things. I fall in love with the quiet
of the morning, the pinpricks of light glowing
from under the blanket of night, and the way
faces pass in a crowd. There is a certain taste
of a late night milkshake after hours of neon
light exploration with company. The way I

asked for a simple teddy bear for Christmas, and keepsake every birthday card since I was a child. I hope that these simple things are what I forever love about life, for then I will be happy no matter where I find myself.

As a writer I have found that these are the things that I love to depict in every poem, writing every way life would bring me the lines. My journal is full of small, interesting notes I have seen in my life. They ranged from the way a woman rushed across the pavement in heels to seeing a baby resting in the arms of his mother. I could never decide if it was the look in someone's eye, or the way a touch swept across skin, but I found the senses hit even when they were not mine. I write anthems to all the things we forget in the rush, in the panic, in the pain. I found that even within themes it is the everyday that dust the heart with emotion. Imprint the beauty of a simple life worth living in each line.

So, when life riddles you with struggles, when you question it all, be a flaneur. Travel and watch, note and see. Listen, not simply hear, and life will give you an abundance. Step out of your shoes, and challenge yourself as a writer. You are capable of grasping some of the sand grains that slide between your fingertips and create art that would be as rich as any life you lead.

Always Will

"I will always love you more, won't I?"

"Um... Well... Is that really a bad thing?"

"Sort of."

"But why?"

"Because I am selfish."

"You're not selfish. I hardly ever see you be selfish. And never when it comes to me."

"Because. I love you, and I love you so wholly that it is almost unfair that it is only one way. You see, when you are away you do not miss me in the way I miss you. You will never pause after something happens and think that you wish I were there, you will revel in that happiness alone. You do not need me there to fully appreciate it."

"And you need me there to appreciate yours?" he asked.

"Most times, no. But sometimes, when I feel like I'm ready to burst, I deflate because you are not there when I turn around."

"But that is scary, isn't it? To love someone that won't let you appreciate your happiness?"

"It isn't that I can't appreciate it. Not exactly... It is that I know I am not as happy as I could be..."

She trailed off, shuffling next to him. He tried to keep her under his arm.

She finally continued:

"You have to understand that when something amazing happens, you are the first person I want to tell. When something makes me angry, you are the person I want to rant to, and have you cheer me on when I curse my coworkers. I don't want to cry alone anymore."

"You don't have to." He said as he smiled at her.

"I don't want to smile alone, either."

"I want you to be there for me when I have those things, too."

"But for you it's different."

He was silent.

"It always will be."

"But will you still be at the church tomorrow?"

"Yes."

"Even if you love me more?"

"Yes, I'll be there. In white."

29 February 2016

Have you ever loved something so much that you never had to even think about whether you did or not? That's how I love him.

All The Songs Became About You

There are so many things
I hope I do not forget about you.
Like how on our first date
you did that really cheesy move
of pointing something out to have a chance
to loop your arm with mine.
And how much I loved it.
I never got to tell you that.
Or how much I loved the way
you would drum on your steering wheel
to all the music you liked.
I loved the way you lit candles,
with the insistence that I never look,
just so I can open my eyes and

find the light in the darkness.
I remembered that day on the bridge,
I remember those nights in your car,
I remember the dreams I had beside you
in bed.
I couldn't tell you when,
but somewhere along the line,
All the songs became about you,
And it all made sense.

The night you held me as I cried,
the times you let me in,
the restless nights together.
I don't know how many of those things
meant something to you.
It's ironic how much it hurts;
even if you saw it coming.
It's scary how you can be haunted
by someone who is still alive.
I showered you with texts to say
goodnight,
I peppered you with apologies
for the things I could not do,
things I failed to do,
or just being who I was.
And I gazed at you
with a constant yearning
that I now realize you do not have for me.
I knew you didn't love me,
but I dangerously adored you anyways.
All the songs became about you,
And it all made sense.

I watched you slip away,
one less word at a time.
I watched you pull away,
without even a kiss goodbye.
I wanted to say "don't leave me,"
But I'm so tired of begging people to stay.
When I said have a good day,
get home safe,
sweet dreams,
I was saying I love you.
You mattered to me so much
that those feelings started to steal
the meaning of everything else.
Now,
I don't think I can think of them
the same now that you're gone.
All the songs became about you,
And it all made sense.

I'm starting to learn that
if things are messy,
or pieces of you don't get put back right,
they are going to hurt, either way.
So, don't say you didn't want to hurt me.
I never realize the last time
is the last time -
It arrives and all I could think of is
all those things I wish I could have one
more time.
When you made your decision,
when I left in tears,

my heart was filled
with questions and confessions,
ones that will never be spoken,
the hardest word to swallow is almost.
And all the songs became about you,
And it all made sense.

Almosts

A poet once said it hurts to think we have failed to reach just good enough so many times that we crafted a word for it.

Almost is the hardest word to swallow, I wrote, as I sat there crying. It pained and stabbed. Prodding me with could-have-beens.

Almost reached the bar, almost said hello. Almost been there, but not quite get there.

In the back of my mind it is almosts that haunt me. They mock me and sit there with their six short letters. Their tales looping around my heart.

Here where the time has yet to pass, it is almost that has yet to come every time. Every time it is almost that has always slipped right out of my hands.

Standing here I wish for something more, I wish for something that could take me away from my almosts, where they are no longer evil to me.

It is the almost smile that pulls on his lips, the playful one that still reaches his eyes that reminds me that there are so many things that defeat almosts.

It is the time that has passed that stand out, the time we lived through to get here. It is the chance to remember the fact that we did it.

We walked across that stage, we have stories to tell, we have another postcard to send.

It is fifty thousand words that are finally on the page, and the laughter that escaped when our smiles were just at almost.

Almost, you cruel and beautiful thing, you will keep haunting me. But he lit candles for me, and I can find the light at the end of the tunnel.

He lit candles for me, and its chance and being has made a flashlight to the future of every ending.

I can't wait to say goodbye to every almost in the back of my mind. Even to the ones that will always be there.

I will say I love you, I will say hello, I will make it to the finish line, I will complete that poem.

Because there is beauty in being able to

tell those who are gone that I lived, and sometimes it makes it feel as though my almosts are quite okay.

Almost, I dare you to know that there is nothing wrong with being incomplete.

Almost, feel free to meet me, because I will walk each of you to the end of the line, heartbreaking and somber, you will make it with me to *"we made it."*

For My Sister With Anxiety

This is how you breathe:
Breathe in, 1 second,
breathe out, 2 seconds;
repeat.

This is how you get rid of excess energy in
a healthy way:
You run,
you dance to loud music,
you scream into your pillow when no one
is around.

This is how you stop from scratching at
your skin during a panic attack:

You rub your hands together,
you play a game on your phone,
you play with a pen,
you draw on your skin wherever you want
to scratch.
You can even play with your hands,
just don't scratch.
Do not scratch.
Your friends will get annoyed when they
see you scratch.
Your friends will yell at you and get
frustrated with you when they see you
scratch.
Do not scratch –
Your friends will pull your hands away –
I told you not to scratch.

This is how you get lost in your head
without being rude:
get a drink of water,
take a sip –
look as though you are contemplating.
Look out the window,
look somber like you're in a movie.
Have a moment.

This is how you write;
honestly,
sloppy,
and self-discover through a pen.

This is what you eat when you are sad:

chocolate is always recommended,
ice cream because the myths of women are
very true sometimes,
and grilled cheese
just the way Papa made it.

This is what you eat when you are happy:
chocolate because it makes you feel the
same way you do when you are in love,
ice cream because it gives you the right
kind of sweet,
and grilled cheese
just the way Papa made it.

This is how you hide how sad you are:
you smile just the same.

This is how you love:
You do it in all the wrong ways,
because that is the only way we know how.
Do not be afraid to love in permanent ink;
cautiously,
with shaky hands and tender words.
Waiting,
waiting,
hoping,
loving.

This is how you explain how you feel:
broken words and hard truths.

This is how you help your younger sister:
the best way you can;
openly,
whether you stammer or fret
you do it with your whole heart.

This –
this mess –
is how you live
happily with anxiety.

I found that there are many things women ask for in a love. Other women demand money, power, or adventure. All I pray for is that he is patient, and plead that he will love me.

In The Right Way

I have to remember it is not love that has hurt me; but someone who could not love me in the right way. Maybe that lesson will lessen the fear of falling in love.

I have spent the last few years in love with love. My high school sweetheart was the perfect man I could have asked to be beside me when he was. The type of man you would imagine when you were young. He was in love with me. The kind of love you didn't have to question because you were never uncertain of it. He would remember all the little things about me. He knew when I was sad without my telling, and he knew how to cherish the moments we were happy. We shared moments that were no one else's. I remember how, on nights I could not sleep from anxiety, he would call me and sing to me over the phone until I fell asleep on the other line. I realized now my love ended because I was not ready for a love like his. With my high school sweetheart it was I who could not love him in the right way.

Then I think of the love I have now. He is so many things that I am still learning. It is sad how the first time I thought "I love him," it was immediately followed by curses to myself at my mistake.

I knew that I f**ked up.

I had not planned on falling for him. Yes, I liked him, but that was good because of all the time we spent together. But to love, and to love him, is petrifying. It is shameful to think of love as scary. As I think about my high school sweetheart and the lullabies over the phone, I try to think about the things that are special with this new love. I think about those moments where I open up to him, those peaceful moments where my hand rests on his in the car. I keep thinking about the way I curl into his side. It is ironic - and slightly moronic - to think of these things because they can be done with anyone. They are simple things that can be replicated and done over and over again. They are not solely ours. We have done them a million times before with other people, and chances are we may do them again with someone else. Yet to me, when I am in those moments and I think back on them, I cannot help but think those are the moments I know I love him. I think it when he glimpses at me while working and breaks into that smile. I think it when he is quietly reading. I think it when 24 hours is just too much for him and his sigh is heavy, and all I can do is be there.

I thought it as he sat there breaking my heart. That was when I realized I had made him question whether I love him. I was not loving him in the right way.

It is funny how when you have been hurt in love and you fall in love again, every reason you have for loving that person is both enough and not, all at once. I can give every reason for why I love him, but I know as I say them they sound trivial. Then I think of me and who I am, and how it is always the little things that make me happy. Those little things are everything to me, they are what make my life worth living. So, why should I not love someone for the little things?

Maybe that is why I am so willing to love so many times. Maybe that is why I am so willing to try again. I want to love in the right way. I want to try. I know my love does not love me, but I also know he is scared to love just like everyone else. I know fear. I know I am okay with loving him, and being happy with him in this moment. I want to try again because when I look back I want to know I tried with every bit of love I had. I am willing to see where this love goes - and if he is willing then I'm okay. A dear friend of mine once told me "hurt people hurt people," and I always understood what they meant. So, as I sat there while my love broke my heart, I knew he hurt me and I knew he was hurting.

Growing up my dad taught me the man you end up with will not be the one who gives you butterflies every time you hold his hand, but the man who makes you feel safe and calm. What is scary about my love now is so often he is both. We all adore love that is messy, that is filled with heartache and struggle. Our hearts have always been sadistic and addicted to the taste of love. So, why would we ever want to keep ourselves from a love like that? Just to be safe? To be overprotective of our bruised hearts? Are we all so hardened by the world? We must learn despite the pain and loss - despite the parts of you that are shredded and did not get put back right - the you that is left is capable and deserving of that love. If they are not both then you are robbing yourself of a love you should feel, not just one you should receive.

People told me never to cross oceans for those who would not jump puddles for you. I sit here, in love, and think the only thing I know is this: Do not listen to those people. Cross oceans, travel the world, give all the pieces of you like handouts on street corners. Love, love in every way you can. Love until it hurts; love even after it hurts. Do it all so you know that you tried everything you could, know there was nothing left you could have done, there was nothing left of you to give. You should live as though you are in love with everything. Therefore, when you are in love it will tickle the parts of you that taste the wanderlust on your tongue. When you are not you should live and love as though it will happen at any moment. Let every grand gesture speak for life and people. Prove your love in all the ways you can count. Love is about so much more than loving. It is about wanting someone, wanting them, choosing them, day after day.

People should love in the same way that they should write; insistently, fervently, *forever*.

Heart Strings

People will speak of the day they met as the day the Earth stood still in each other's eyes - everyone said they could feel the pull of their love. The whirlwind romance was documented in photo albums and my mother's sloppy hand-written journal entries that have become my bible. There is always a problem with love, however. Humans are so fiercely mortal. Whether we die, or we leave, mortality takes us away so simply. Sometimes our mortality makes us fall in love with someone who could only be there for a few months. Love seems to come in comets; flashes of fire and passion, arriving so quickly and gone by morning. When my mother met my father, they fell to the concrete and through the Earth. And when my father left they said my mother's heart bent and bend in this way and that. Some recount how she sat in her chair, her belly growing with me, and felt the throbbing in her chest, the butterflies dying in her stomach one by one. I swear, I cradled each one of them as they fell.

The story goes, when I was born, and my mother took one look at my face, she saw my father's eyes which made her heartstrings break. They snapped and gnarled, and she died on the hospital bed having gave birth to the daughter of the love of her life who did not love her back. The doctors would describe how they stood around worried why I did not cry. For three days I did not echo a peep. Nurses tell me my newborn tears slid down my cheeks in haunting silence.

As it turns out, I inherited my mother's heartbreak. At times I cannot help but wonder if it was my mother's heartbreak I inherited or my parents actions that broke my own heart. Explanations are made no use of however, especially in matters of reality. My heartstrings were broken, and for an infant that was surely going to mean death. There seemed to be nothing anyone could do, and plans were immediately made to make me as comfortable as possible. I try to image the hospital that day; a place where births are meant to balance the grief of death, and here I had been ready to disturb this balance with the death of both mother and child. I imagine the color being blacks and blues.

It was Theresa who had stepped up to the staff and demanded she take charge. In little time my tiny chest was opened on the surgical table, the body of a baby barely reaching five pounds was overwhelmed and drowned in the stainless instruments of medicine. Theresa worked restlessly for six hours. The method was simple micro needle and thread, far too many stitches to count; just like that Theresa had worked wonders on me, my heartstrings sewn back together. Her complex surgery granted her a goddaughter to take care of for the next eighteen years.

While my family looks at me as either a miracle or the ghost of my mother, Theresa was the constant in my life who took care of me as a singular being with my own identity. From before I understood what Theresa was saying, she relayed the rules to me, the ones that would keep my heart healthy.

"You must watch your temper, you must replace your string every year, you must have a diet high in fruits and vegetables, and you must keep your temper as best as you can." Theresa would mumble these to me as bedtime lullabies.

Yet there was one rule I granted to myself, the cause of all the documented cases of broken heart syndrome, and I told myself this rule every time Theresa would go.

I must not fall in love.

27 March 2016

There are people out there who are willing to go through life with you, and you're a charmer for sure. In the end it is really you who gets to choose that. You have to be willing to stick around, too.

The Color Brown

"I had fallen in love with a color."
- Maggie Nelson, *Bluets*

When I was younger I would pout and whine to my father my complaints of not inheriting grey or blue eyes like my baby sisters. I would look in the mirror and wish for anything but brown eyes. Pulling at the strands of my hair I wished I were a ginger, to have a fiery mane that drew the eye. I wanted to embody what I loved about my favorite colors, to be bright and lively. My mother once told me the reason she decided to have a child by my father was because she wanted a baby with blonde hair and blue eyes, instead she ended up with me. Little does my mother know I'm quite disappointed myself.

Self-expression has been my savior. My wardrobe is smattered with color, reds and greens. I rebelled against my genes and dyed my hair blues and pinks. I've etched color into my skin and painted my lips every morning. I found no beauty in blacks, whites or browns.

It seems ironic, how ordinary he is, all the ways the simple strings thread him together. There were many old things, left behind from a time he did not know. There were parts of him made up of street corners he remembered as a child, a product of a life I know well enough to understand. They resemble small circles, rings in a tree trunk that tell where you have been. All the simple things that make up all that is him were all the things that made me stay. It has become unsurprising that one of my favorite aspects of who he is are those brown eyes.

Something that has been what I wanted to change the most about myself has become what captivates me time again. I found my thoughts in circles often enough to become acquainted with their shape long after they have closed for the night. Had I not watched as they became halos in the sun I may not have learned how the Earth has given much of itself to each of us. Those eyes that enrich whatever they seem to come across, taking in everything they see. They are as wanderlust as the breeze and steady as a tree.

When a supernova occurs the elements that create everything we find in our universe was made. It is these elements we are all made up of. From here you can gather that we are all made up of stars. Looking into those golden rays, eclipsed with a port key, I realize for certain brown can never describe eyes, because they were never really just brown. They were always so much more.

His Name Is Joseph

If I should ever have a son, I will name him Joseph. I will name him Joseph because the men in my life, as I was growing up, with this name were angels in disguise. Flawed, imperfect angels that meant well. When Joe died I could tell you the parts of me that went with them, that is an easy thing to understand but a much harder thing to feel. I have waited for those pieces to return. They haven't. Maybe a new Joe will bring light to the world once again, at least I like to think so.

Papa Joe was the angel disguised as a hustler - at least that is how my father described him. I always liked that depiction. Papa was the man who came to the aid of the world. I never learned what the universe did to him that made him believe he is the one who needs to be the good in it. I never heard about his past, and even his birth-given name had been a mystery until the day he passed. He was a reformation. He was a reincarnation of his old self in the same body. Papa, if you had the great chance to know him, was the man who took care of everyone he knew. He was the stepfather who stepped up to the plate. He was the man who if you were distantly related you were family nonetheless. Papa was the man who picked you up from the airport and helped you move your couch. A hard man to describe if not told in a series of stories, each would lighten the heart and each strikingly simple. It was Papa who taught me to love the world. I'm still learning how to do that again after it took him away.

Uncle Joe was my godfather, and he lived up to the title. I spent my youth traveling Catholic schools in New York City, and time after time he would send his money for my schooling. He would send his wishes and pieces of his heart across highway miles. Every time I saw Uncle Joe attached to his ring finger was great aunt Laura. She never looked more alive as she was beside him, it was a constant miracle to see in a dying woman. He shared small glances with her from across dinner tables, and they suffered each other's families every holiday. We would joke that the poor Irishman had put himself through the family of crazed Puerto Rican women. Ever patient, and ever in love, it was no secret why he stayed. It was their love that taught me to fall in love with the simplicity of holding hands across the front seats of the car. Uncle Joe was a man of deep love. That's why it came as no surprise after my aunt passed, Uncle Joe followed. Two months after the love of his life passed, he died of a broken heart. Uncle Joe, the man who showed me how to love. I hope one day I may find my own "Joe" to show me all that love.

I have learned so much love from these two incredible men. I hope by naming my son Joseph it will bring him the qualities of these two great men in the same way Irish folklore tells us the effects of naming a child after someone who has passed. I hope that he has the patience of a man who thinks he has all the time in the world, and lives in a way of a man who still knows that he can only do so once. I pray my son is a Joe that can love the people in his life in the simple moments. I hope my little Joe will become a man of truth laced words and many actions of proof. May Joe have as much love in his life. If my son Joseph does not hold their qualities, then I at least hope he becomes another amazing Joe into someone's life. Let Joseph be a person the world needs.

Rebecca Perez, *My Dear*

When my daughter comes home for Christmas and I see a spark in her eyes it will remind me of you, and how you always use to tell me the world was stock piled with second chances.

The Truth About Love

A Learning Experience from Broken Hearts

Often when we are in our beds somber over a broken heart we ask ourselves why we find ourselves in these positions. We ask ourselves why is it this way? Are we constantly so misunderstood that we find ourselves alone? For some of us we ask why we waited for the person in the first place, whether it was for them to get themselves together or simply waiting for the moment that they would finally love us back. We have fears that build up from these questions to ourselves, the people around us, and the people who we have relationships with.

In reality we must all first realize that there are actually two vastly different types of love. Being loved and loving. When we think of relationships we always bring to mind the images of someone loving us; being understood, having a constant companion, and having something that is supposed to be wholly unconditional. But we are never truly ready to be in a loving relationship until we are ready to put aside these idealized beliefs and be the ones on the giving end of the partnership. We must learn to love in the way that a parent does: constantly giving our love without ever expecting to be given back in any significant way. We must love in a way that almost demands that we sometimes set aside our own expectations for the needs of another. To love as adults we must learn, perhaps for the first time, to put someone else ahead of ourselves.

Nowadays, some of us slip into pitfall of worrying over loving someone more than we love ourselves. However, as adults this is exactly what can end up happening when we enter the paternal way of loving another person. While it may not always be the case, it is known to happen, and happen frequent enough. The true failing on our part is loving someone who does not in turn help us love ourselves. It's like when our partner mentions how much they like our eyes or the shape of our nose and the next time we turn to the mirror we may have a bit more fondness for them because of it. In this way we learn to love our kindness, our quietness, and our nerdy tendencies. It is through our partner many times that we begin to like all of our vast intricacies, hyperboles, nuances, and contradictions. While it is okay to love someone more than ourselves, we must remember for them to be deserving of our love they cannot be toxic to us. They must help us love ourselves, even in miniscule ways, and helping us grow in who we are and who we are to become.

Some of us may have even already learned these lessons; we spent our time in love with someone and waited for them. There are many reasons we may wait for someone, but the two most cited have always been to get their lives together or for them to fall in love with us too. The truth is when we wait for someone we have made the ultimate decision ourselves and that is that this person is worth waiting for. We love them because of the way they kiss our cheek or learned who we are. We love them because they have made memories with us and made us feel cared for at some point or another. They made us believe. Because of all of these things, and the selfless love we have for them, we felt they are worth the wait. In situations like these, when it turns sour, that it is our partners who are not ready to love like a parent. Perhaps, it is because they are competitive and they strive for the best, a mythical thing that simply does not exist. It does not mean that these people were not worth the wait, it just means that the waiting must end at some point. When that time comes, if they love you as well, then it can lead down a road for both of you to grow and continue on together. If the wait ends without them by your side it is important to remember that we were not wrong. They still did all those things, we still had all those memories, and we still grew from the experience of loving that person. We must remember in this time that we must not be afraid to love someone else again because they are not a continuation or repeat of this past love.

That brings us to our fears about love. Especially once we have been hurt, we begin to fear not only loving someone but being loved. Many of us are afraid of loving another person because it is so vulnerable, brings up the past, changes us, and is unequal. We are aware of how much we have to trust another person and feel exposed to them for them to even get the chance to truly know us in the way that we hope. It's when we start to do this that we realize how much of the past has to come up when we fall in love again, and that can scare us for many reasons. Our pasts are not generally something we are going to be proud or happy about. If we are not ready we will fear love because we are still unwilling to let go of our own egos and selfishness, we are not ready to change or love in the way we are expecting to be loved. Some people, however, are more afraid of being loved. We do not know how to take something seemingly too good to be true and not flee from it. What we realize, even if we are not the ones loving, any relationship requires work and there is someone else's feelings on the line. Those afraid of being loved will resist and pull away. If we are afraid of being loved we often become defensive and refuse to let things get too deep, whether by leaving or keeping ourselves at a distance from the person who loves us. It will always be something that makes us slower to love or hesitate often in a relationship more than those who are far more willing to love than we are, and what we will be in need of is someone who is willing to wait for us. We need someone who is willing to help us learn to accept love.

When we are ready to love though we will start to take a look at the things that keep love away. The truth is that we will never find the right person- for they do no exist. There is no perfect person, there is no one. In fact we must admit to ourselves that we will never be that for another person. We must admit to ourselves that there is something wrong with us, as there is with everyone else. Because of this we will never be fully understood, we will sometimes still feel alone, we will even find ourselves questioning ourselves in moments until the next when we are ready to get out of our own heads. We must, in the end, give up on perfection. We will need to silence our inner critic. We will learn to ignore it when it tells us to avoid when it gets uncomfortable or baring, and ignore it when it makes us second guess ourselves and the people around us. Just the same, we must learn to silence the critic in times where it has made us too judgmental towards those around us, the one that jumps at any fault a person may have and use it as evidence to run in the other direction. We must give people a real chance. We must challenge ourselves as to why we even have our defenses in the first place and remember that we can never truly allow someone to love us if we are keeping them out. Our walls are no longer constructive to us in our relationships. Needing to be open and vulnerable is as necessary to love as it is to being loved. Most of all, we need to allow ourselves to feel our emotions. We must be ready to feel all the spectrums of love, from its passions and bliss to the pain and sadness.

In all, there is but one thing that we must learn that though love is work and hard, it is so infinitely selfless when we are creatures of excessive selfishness, it will change you and you get to decide whether you are willing to do so.

Existential Crisis

"Am I a writer or a minority writer?"
- Jaswinder Bolina, *Writing Like a White Guy*

I was recently asked by a professor in the English department to come and speak to a Woman's Literature class. The professor asked me to read some of my work and then continue by touching on subjects of poetry, the process of writing, and how being a woman has impacted my writing. There was just one problem; I wasn't quite sure myself how being a woman has influenced my writing.

I have always been an avid reader; a dedicated soul to the printed word. I own just over three hundred books. It was not until recently where I began to pay attention to the writer at all. A book has always been its own story, the writer was separate. After all, once a book is published it belongs to the reader. In lieu of that, would it not make sense to my mind then to take the writer out of the equation completely? The names on the covers have always just been letters, and I never sought to think who it was behind those names. Three years ago as I was coming into my own ideas of equity, I realized, as so many others do, that I cannot simply do the talking. I must put my beliefs into practice. As a feminist this meant I had to unravel the sexism within myself, my own behavior and habits. In my bookish world this idea meant I had to start paying attention to those names on my books.

In my first count after this realization the ratio for my collection was one book written by a woman for every four written by a man. These days, I've begun to do the same when it comes to diversity, and that is another problem in and of itself. But what did any of this matter? Why was a collection of books meant to be diverse and why could I not be comfortable with it unless it was?

The problem was this: who exactly was being heard?

In this world where the idealized "literature" is dominated by the old white cis male there are millions of voices not being represented. If there is one thing we have learned in our history it is representation matters. The vision of someone like us ahead propels us forward into fields and dreams we did not think would be ours for the taking.

I have always been in love with writing. The great phrase is if you do not find the book that you wish to read, then you must write it yourself. There have been many stories that I have been in great want for, and notebooks and hard drives have been buried with my writing. Being a writer did not change my desire for diversity, it simply gave me a small way to implement my ideas. When I thought of how being a woman impacted me as a writer, I thought of my identity. What did I say I was? Was I a woman writer or was I a writer who is a woman? I challenged the idea of being more than my stereotype, and I challenged the idea that I will be anything other than one who was inspired by words.

I chose my identity as a bisexual minority woman writer with the thought of all those I could inspire, where I can stand alongside as representation of a much larger community. Teaching a Women's Literature class for a day brought more than questions on my process of writing, it made me want to extend an olive branch. Being all these things at once made me realize I never have to choose, I am all this and more.

Holy

"Sometimes they come out so gay, they're flaming."

This was the joke that was said across the room when they decided their opinion mattered in someone else's marriage.

I remember listening in as my body curled around Gatsby, as I heard someone else say, "they can have a partnership if they want, but don't call it marriage. That is a holy thing."

I couldn't help but wonder when marriage became synonymous with religious. Sitting in City Hall to get a marriage license only feels like church because of those perfect identical rows. But it's far less filled with hypocrisy these days, I have noticed.

Marriage, they say, is supposed to be holy; so let me tell you this: If given the chance I will treat your body like a chapel. I will praise you every Sunday from dawn to dusk with the lips I use to pray, on my knees while you scream out to God. I hope that is holy enough to please them.

I want to love like my grandmother, who loved a woman like Joseph loved Mary. Someone so imperfect, so human, brave enough to love someone who already knows God. But they were never allowed in a church as they truly are. It makes me realize how much a child can betray someone's memory.

I sat there curled around Gatsby, thinking how the church raised me to be nice and quiet, but on Sunday all I hear is noise. Screams to God for forgiveness for their sins. But I am not screaming with them. I know that God cannot be found in a congregation, but in the humanity of another.

Love sounds a lot like God these days, and I hope my love is enough for you.

My Skin: Take Pride In It

The color of my skin.
The color of the surface of my skin.
Is not as white as yours.
The color of the surface of my skin
tinted like windows,
mocking the sun,
creating artificial nightfall creeping across
my skin.

My skin,
superficially dirty.
The more you stare at my velvet skin
the more you grow in desire to
wash my skin.

To scrub and scrape the filth off of my skin.
You mock me,
You mock me and taunt me.
Because my skin is not as lovely.
Not as lovely,
As the ivory porcelain
stretched across your body,
Like a marble statue staring down at me.
You dread.
You dread because you want to rid yourself
of the ancestral bond
You so desperately want to leave behind.
The one I take in with so much pride.
My pride in my skin.

My skin,
Like the sun couldn't stop kissing my skin.
My skin,
Like a chocolate bar broken open to reveal
luscious caramel.
My skin,
The color of brown sugar
and I'm sure taste just as sweet.
My skin
Your skin
The one you take so much shame in.
His skin, Her skin
Not like our skin.
But still I could never find myself
to be ashamed
of my beautiful cinnamon brown
skin.

My New Favorite F Word

Feminism is my new favorite F word
But it's funny how furious it makes some
  folks
I've spent hours trying to explain to a
  childhood friend
Why Feminism is still needed,
And he asked what could it do for him?
It's funny how something for women still
  became about men.

I try to remember the first time I became a
  feminist
But it seems silly to think,
Because as a woman I feel like I've always
  been.
It was the wrapping paper of the dolls I got
  for Christmas,
And the surprise from some family members

When I said I wanted a microscope.
It was the bitter taste in the back of my
    throat
When, as 12 year old Catholic school girl,
We were catcalled by 30 year olds.

I remember thinking how unfair it was
That my boyfriend of 15 had more freedom
    than me;
Even when I was 17.
And everyone kept making fun of me,
Saying I was a cougar,
But he was stud.
They use to tell us girls we were lucky,
Because we got away with being late to class
With the batting of our eyelashes.
No one understood the fear
Of walking down crowded hallways
With too many hands.

We return to lunchroom tables
With boys giggling over women
Who travel in packs to bathrooms,
Little do we even remember
It started because we were taught
We have safety in numbers.
Because we heard of the horror stories
Of men who waited in bathroom stalls.
Haunted by tales of rape jokes gone wrong.
Newspaper articles of women who realize
No was the wrong answer.

I realize now my feminism was embedded in
The anger I had as men tell me
Take it as a compliment.
And others kept saying I am so exotic.
There are men who use my body as public
  property,
And use my clothes as examples of a
  welcome matt.
Teenage boys pin up our half naked bodies as
  decoration,
And men who hang us around their arm for
  the same reason.
I am a feminist when I am asked
Whether I want to be successful or a parent,
And understand
Men are never forced to choose between the
  two.
How odd it is men cannot wear pink,
Because god forbid they seem feminine.
And magazines can't stop selling us ways for
  women to lose weight.

I remember my uncle demanding my cousin
  to punch him the face,
So he knew when she went out door
She was capable of defending herself.
I remember how my sisters watched as their
  mother's new boyfriend
Was brought to prison in handcuffs,
Because they sat there as they watched their
  mother get beaten.
I remember their faces when they told me he

returned.
Sometimes the keys between our knuckles
Aren't for the stranger in the alley way.
Statistics tell us they are more likely to be
For the man who crept down our hallways.
I am a feminist when I remember
1 in 6 women will experience rape
And I am 1 of 7 granddaughters.

Feminism is my new favorite F word,
And I understand now it's not meant to be
    popular.
It's meant to start breaking down barriers,
And shattering glass ceilings.
The only people it seems to make sense to
Are the people who claim it.
We don't always realize it
But labels are good sometimes,
Because it's breaking the silence.
We have to remember this isn't about
Your mothers, wives, sisters or daughters,
It is about part the human population.
Feminism is my new favorite F word,
Especially because still too many people
    don't like it.

Goodbye NYC

Dear New York City,

The drive tends to be rather long, something therapeutic. Watching the window from the passenger seat, hopefully with some good company as the passenger. I don't know where I would be driving to yet; maybe I'll be off to Manchester, somewhere I've only been in passing. Maybe I'll be on my way to Pennsylvania, somewhere I spent summer every year as a kid, somewhere I am intimately connected with. Nonetheless, I would be going somewhere with trees and changing seasons, a place where I can sit on the floor of my home in the sun and drink coffee as I listen to the birds in the morning. New York City, one thing I will not miss is the traffic instead of birds.

When I leave, I know it will be to call somewhere else home. I will carry your accent, and I will carry with me Broadway show tunes, but in the end you will be my childhood. My future will rest in the palm of another city. New York City, be sure to know it is not because I no longer love you that I am leaving. We have been an affair, the first love - the love of my life. Valentines are made out in your shape. My dreams will taste of Yankee Stadium funnel cake, dancing in neon and LED lights. The sounds of The Heights will fall from my lips every day. New Year's Eve will be dim compared to Times Square.

New York City, since the moment we met when I opened my eyes you were so certain to show me everything to become the person that I needed to be. You cradled me with concrete and glass buildings. You toughened me with scrapes and bruises, and humbled me with the streets. New York City, you were rough on me. You gave me nights when my asthma choked me and scary news stories. There was a lot of the same; Chinese takeout, bodega dreams, and the rush.

New York City, you gave me the rush. A rush that flowed through my veins with too much oxygen. I feel light. I feel explosive. I walk your sidewalks speckled with dry, grey gum and glitter. I walk like in a dream, and that's how I like to remember you. The taste of illegal barbeque in parks and the feeling in my gut as I swing just too high. When I have a milkshake I will think of my diner, and the late nights with my best friends. I will be haunted by the kiss on 5th Avenue, and smile at the memory of the kiss on the Brooklyn Bridge. I will return for your museums, and poetry slams. There will be days where I will drive for hours to return to the restaurants my step father worked at across the city. I will remember my home; and you were my first.

New York City, you have given me years of love letters with typos I have ignored. Now that I am older I am ready to start writing my own. Maybe one day I will return, but until then the heart must grow fonder apart. New York City, I tell you goodbye for now, because there is still so much I have left to do. I want to teach, I want to share knowledge. I want to spend some peaceful mornings with the song birds. I have to show my sisters how it is done.

New York City, goodbye, my love.

From my new place to belong,
Your Dear Old Friend.

Spring

Spring must be the season of poetry,
When Shakespeare yearned for a comparison
to a summer's day whispering its coming
arrival in the winds of May poppy fields.
It seems as if all the love poems bloom after
basking in April showers.
But I am not a poet.
And while I lay beneath dreaming in verse
and in rhyme,
You will never see someone compare my
scrawl to Keats's *Bright Star* shinning in the
warm night sky,
And though I stand before you, my legs keep
shaking, and my hands keep stuttering, and
my self-confidence can only be measured out
into teaspoons
Mixed into my poetry and still, somehow,

tastes funny in my mouth.

Spring is the season of poetry.
 Just like newborn babies being brought onto
this Earth, my poems take life with their
first breath of air.
Maybe I am not a poet.
Everyone likes to take it as a hobby of mine,
"My words are pushing daisies," they tell me
"You better have a Plan B."
But all these bees seem to be doing for me is
populate the garden of my gut as I stand
here on stage.

Spring is the season of poetry,
Because as these lights shine down on me it
feels like the sun melting away my fears
from the long, brisk winter cold;
A glow building within as I share my stories
that have been longing to be told.
I am a poet.
I need not a judge to tell me so;
I need not an English teacher's opinion to
tell me so.
I am a poet.
And spring is the season for poetry.

Everyday Poetry

"Whoever is a poet is one always, and
continually assaulted by poetry."
- Jorge Luis Borges, *Blindness*

*Assault; verb, a physical or strong
verbal attack.*

It is no wonder that we believe so strongly
in the tortured artist. If it is words or colors
that chase after us, that beat us until we
know nothing but their names, then it is no
wonder we are painted in Picasso's blues and
yellows. I have reminisced over past poetry,
and replayed the recordings of performances
of a young girl I still do not recognize as
myself. I have come to realize words are
snowballs, there is a momentum behind their

lifetime, building into this mass of paper and flesh colored ink.

How often does our poetry become us? Where we see the lights dance, the way a hand laces with another, the scent of burning sugar. The way a waiter gestures can take up a page in a journal, and napkins are used quite often. Being a poet often means a different lens to view the world, we see things in gradients. We are inspired by the everyday.

So often it is where I hear someone say they are not a writer, they are not a hero. We are all heroes, as long as we are living. We are all poets, so long as we are writing our story.

Poetry has made sure I never grow tired of the night sky, of thunderstorms. Poetry has made sure I never tire of dancing in the rain, of singing off key. Poetry has made me fall in love. I am battered by the ways the songbirds sing in the quiet, early mornings, the puff of clouds into thought bubbles. I am awed every time by the galaxies cream makes in my coffee. Poetry, my insistent lover, has inspired me to love the small, beautiful things.

29 October 2015

He said if I want you to be special I can't
treat you like everyone else. I made sure
since then that I always did the same.

An Open Letter: To The Last Person I Will Ever Love

To The Last Person I Will Ever Love,

If you are reading this and you think for just a moment this could, should, might, maybe, or possibly be about you, please keep reading. I have been in love three times in my life and it has taught me one thing if nothing else; a chance coincidence can change everything. So, if I am homeward bound and you are reading this, know I will always be here waiting for you to join me. You will know what to do from there.

You see, I have been looking for you for a very long time, and I have come to the conclusion you are either out there somewhere riding a turtle's back, lost and confused, or you are playing a cruel game of hide and seek with my consciousness and I just don't know you are there yet. I wonder often if we have met already. Are you in eyes I know well or the coy smile of a stranger on the subway? Have I sat beside you hundreds of times and never noticed?

I imagine you sitting there, reading your novel, curled into the question mark. Trying to give the answers to soften people in this hardening world. I imagine you will feel like home, and it will not be love at first sight but a deep, satisfying familiarity; like when I know I will just think "so, it's you." I imagine that you will make this woman feel beautiful for the first time in the largest part of a long while. I imagine you standing there not having to forgive me for my vices, but helping me to overcome them. With you I will no longer feel like I need to start every sentence with the word sorry.

Somehow, you will arrive despite my obstacle course of anxiety; taking great care of my whimsical heart in your hands because, in the end, I know only you will never break it. Please know my promises are laugh lines, happily permanent.

I promise I will never give up on you. Everything I have ever let go of has claw marks on it, so never assume you are easy to surrender to the wind. Fear not, for we will no longer have to play coasters for half empty hearts, because I will give you my all.

My darling, I have been told you only ever know someone in the age you have met them, but even so I want to know you. I want to know who you were before the world told you who to be. I want to know what you would do if you were not afraid. How many times did you draft the list of your imperfections? How many times did you forgive them? I will learn every way to make your smile easier. I will know the little ticks you do; what you do when you are overthinking, when you concentrating, when you are upset. I hope I can know every broken piece of you; and I will adore all the ways in which you are broken for it gives me more of you to love. I will never ask of you the impossible, I just ask you to love me in the best way you can. You are like a flower, beautiful simply for existing.

I hope I never dream of you, so I never fill you up to be someone you are not, because you are wonderful as you are. You are made up of flawed splendor I can taste on my tongue. The fingerprints of you will be embedded on me to forever show you were here.

There will be an embrace that puts the pieces of us together; and when we look at each other again we will know. I am sure, even now, I will cry. Partly because I'm sappy and hopeless, but mostly because I think the world would finally return to the colors of childhood. My knees would buckle, and your heart will stutter, stammer, and I will recite poetry to its beat with my lips across yours.

You are enough, you are worth it. Worth every ballad, worth every word, every action. We will be in a love where we understand why they call it falling - because you never really do it on purpose. It always just happens, and you can feel it in your stomach, and chest, and every atom of your body. In fact, I'm sure our very atoms would have been together back when the universe was created, and we have been searching to reunite them ever since. If you can remember back then, way back when we were still stardust, maybe then you will understood how much I love you.

I will show you all the ways in which you are easy to love. We will argue, we will fight, we will have our differences and opinions, and we will make mistakes. But, my darling, you will never be difficult to love. I will always want to be next to you at the end of the day. You may not be everything I was looking for, but you will be everything I waited for.

I will love you in the exact way I have always wanted to be loved.

31 December 2015

He asked me once what I wanted when I died, what I wanted out of life, and I told him I just wanted more happy memories than sad ones.

Afterword

When I was younger I remember sitting in my grandfather's enormous chair with my legs dangling in the air, the folding table placed in front of my with all my school work spread out before me. My grandmother sat at the computer, keeping an eye on me from afar. It wasn't much of a trouble to watch me, as she often did, because I was a quiet child most times. I worked hard and hardly made a peep, but the one thing my grandmother will always remember would be the moment I piped up and asked her a question. "Grandma," I asked, "can I take a break?" Never one to deny me of much, she let me. The next time she turned around she found me curled into the chair reading a book. Surprised, she asked me if I was going to take my break, to which I replied: "I am taking my break, Grandma. I'm reading!" The hilarity of the tale was something that has been retold at family events ever since. A love of reading had been instilled in me since I learned my alphabet, since I got my first library card. Reading was what I did, I rushed to finish all my work in class to go off and do so, when my teachers declared it was quiet reading time I looked up from the book I had already cracked open.

I do not know when reading had transitioned into writing. I only remember thinking: "I would write this differently." From there I went into writing my own work, little short stories and notebooks of novels which were never finished. Pages were a currency in my life, I exchanged life and breath for ink and paper. This currency grew in worth as I got older.

In the beginning I focused on fiction writing, but I had trouble building my own worlds. Upon the discovery of fanfiction, something I had unwittingly been doing for some time, I used the worlds and characters of other works to springboard my stories into existence. What were the things that I would have changed in the story; would the situation change, would the backdrop plot become the main focus, a new setting, a new character? I challenged myself to write out the daydreams I played alongside the books I read. From there I learned the butterfly effect of a story. By the end product I would have a story that would bounce between friends and encouraging teachers for entertainment and test my skills.

It was not until sophomore year of high school that I was introduced to a new form of writing, poetry. When I first walked into the little red trailer the first thing I realized was it was certainly not a traditional class. We were in a large circle, the professors were sitting and they were not the ones who ran the lesson. Amy, Joe and Roland were the odd trio that started up the program. They had the radical notion that they can teach low-income students through literacy and writing in a way that would profoundly change their lives in a way that can break the cycle of poverty and schooling using pedagogy and creative writing. The motto of the program was this: "If you don't learn to write your own life story someone else will write it for you." All of us who have gone through the program take this phrase solemnly because for the first time our voices were being heard. At first my writing was lousy. I cringe now when I read through my first poems. I tried to mimic voices at first, exploring different styles before I slowly began developing my own. Poetry began to take root in my writing, using it as a creative outlet and therapy. I had found a close knit family with people who took care of me in so many ways I could let only them do. I found people who would travel with me in life longer than those years in high school.

The surprises of working in a creative writing course and compiling work for a book was how much of it was a freeing experience. In society we get caught up in what is expected, in pleasing everyone else around us. When it came to our books, our work, we were unbound. An artist is the best thief, one who knows how to hide their influences and make them their own. Writing has always been a passing along of language and ideas scrambled in all the ways we can rearrange the twenty-six letters of the alphabet. All the writers in the class used ideas from published authors we read, and in every class I found myself writing lines from my professor Aimee Herman and my classmates. I look back on those notes when I need inspiration. It is a strange kind of envy when you come across someone who thought of something you wouldn't have, because you are still jubilant that someone shared it with you.

The challenge of writing this book was the challenge I had with every other book I attempted: finishing. The idea that a piece is complete is alien to me. There is always more to add, or a better way of explaining something. Those are only the conceptually based drawbacks. Structurally there are numerous worries to fret over; grammar, order, syntax. Writing becomes a chore easily when it is never fully accomplished. Most times a book is only a baby who has has yet to develop into all it could be.

Lessons as a writer have been the prying of fingers off of work, to give it a chance to ferment into the minds of others and allow the criticism to flourish. I have drifted to other forms of writing, and other genres. Above all, my lessons as a writer has granted me more teachings for my life, which would in turn expand my writing, thus an everlasting cycle.

During the exploration of this book I have come to define what my love is and my downfalls. Now more than ever I have taken notice of the *memento mori* that rears its head with the lives we build, along with the best ways to be so unbelievably alive.

I felt lucky to have come across inspiration in the people around me. I had found great company and those that were determined to express their lives through words - even if only inspired to do so by the due dates of each project. Most of all though, I had been granted motivation to write through the people I have met that evoked all the feelings that have inspired me to write every piece. I am also thankful for my editor, artisan, creative partner, and best friend, for he was as much a part of this book as all the others, and without him it would have never been made. My sister kept me grounded to reality and was a reminder of the family I have and the one I will.

But there was also love. Love, with its passion and grandeur, followed someone who was willing to instill new narratives to tell and challenge me to speak these words I have only ever written before. I am thankful for him. Now, it is all forever held together in binding, hopefully to last longer than even myself and these memories. To remain profound, lasting, and echoing onto the page.